lithgow
balooza readers

W9-AAR-541

Sing, Strum, and Beat the Drum!

By Teresa Domnauer

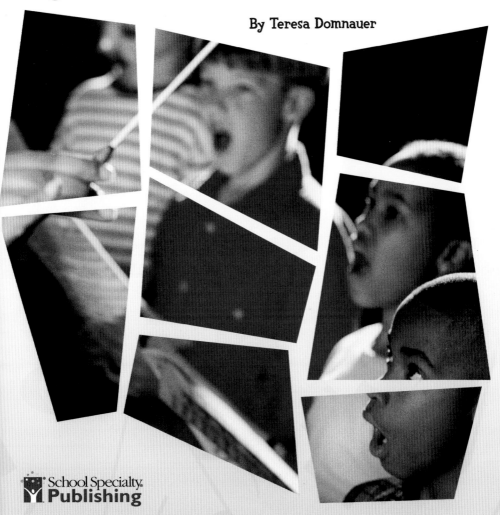

School Specialty Publishing

Send all inquiries to:
School Specialty Publishing
8720 Orion Place
Columbus, OH 43240-2111

ISBN 0-7696-4224-1

1 2 3 4 5 6 7 8 9 10 PHXBK 10 09 08 07 06 05

Table of Contents

Pop Singer

Pop stars devote their lives
to performing music.
They spend many hours in voice
and acting classes.
They often start this training
at a very young age.
Pop singers must have natural talent
and be comfortable on the stage.
They travel the country giving concerts.
Often, these musical stars are away
from home for a very long time.

Farkle Fact

The pop group the Eagles holds the record for the most albums sold in the United States. *Their Greatest Hits 1971–1975* sold 28 million copies!

Rock Guitarist

A rock guitarist must have
talent and be willing to work hard.
The life of a rock guitarist
is a busy one.
Rock guitarists perform in concerts.
They appear in music videos.
They record songs with their bands.
That is not all.
Rock guitarists must practice the guitar,
learn new songs, and meet fans.
They travel long distances to perform
in city after city.

Farkle Fact

Jimi Hendrix was a famous guitarist in the 1960s.
Hendrix is known for making all kinds of new rock-and-
roll sounds on the guitar. He could even play the guitar

Orchestra Member

An orchestra has different
sections of instruments.
Orchestra members must practice with
their section and with the whole orchestra.
Some orchestra members travel
all over the world to perform.
Musicians in an orchestra have years
of training.
They attend a **conservatory**,
which is a special music school.
They spend many hours studying
and practicing their music.

Farkle Fact

Violinist Midori Goto is a very talented musician. By
the time she was 11, Midori was performing with the
New York Philharmonic Orchestra.

Jazz Musician

Like rock musicians and
orchestra members, jazz musicians
center their lives around music.
They practice and write new music.
They often travel from place to place to perform.
Some jazz musicians play instruments,
like the saxophone or the trumpet.
Other musicians, who sing with jazz bands,
are **vocalists**.

Farkle Fact

Wynton Marsalis is one of today's most famous jazz
artists. He comes from a very talented family. His
father and three brothers are also jazz musicians.

Choir Director

Choir directors instruct groups
of people who sing together.
They pick the music that the choirs
will sing.
They set up times for practice.
They listen to singers **audition**.
Choir directors also choose
the best singing voices.
These people are given special parts to sing.
Choirs have different sections,
just like orchestras.
Choir directors help each section sing its part.
They also make sure that all the sections
blend together.

Farkle Fact

The Vienna Boys' Choir has been performing for over 500 years. Its members are 11 to 14 years old. They receive special musical training and spend many months on tour each year.

Conductor

Conductors direct groups of
musicians, such as orchestras.
They choose the music
that these groups will play.
Conductors must be able to read a **score**
of written music.
A score shows the parts that the different
instruments play.
Conductors hold a small **baton** stick in their hands.
They wave the baton to show how softly
or loudly or how quickly or slowly the music
should be played.
The conductor also signals when the musicians
should start and stop playing their instruments.

Farkle Fact

Arthur Fiedler is one of the world's best-known
conductors. He led the Boston Pops Orchestra
for 50 years.

Composer

Composers write music.
They put musical notes together
in patterns.
They choose different rhythms and **pitches**.
They combine **melodies** and **harmonies**
in a creative way.
Some composers write music
for movies and television.
Some composers, like Mozart, wrote music
hundreds of years ago that is still popular today.
Composers study music for many years.
They usually play several instruments,
including the piano.

Farkle Fact

Ellen Taafe Zwilich is an American composer. She was the first woman to receive the Pulitzer Prize in Music. This is a special award that only a few people in the world receive.

Songwriter

Songwriters are musicians
who write popular music,
such as rock-and-roll songs.
Songwriters write the music
and the words to a song.
Many songwriters play the piano
or the guitar as they write their songs.
Some songwriters perform their own songs.
Some write music for other people to perform.
Songwriters write **jingles** for television and radio.
Sometimes, songwriters work in pairs.
In this case, usually one person writes the words
to the song and the other writes the music.

Farkle Fact

John Lennon and Paul McCartney wrote 23 songs
that became number one rock-and-roll hits in the
United States.

Music Store Owner

Music store owners do not need
to play instruments.
But they must know how to run
a business.
Music store owners provide music, instruments,
and other equipment for people to buy.
They order items to stock in their stores.
They track the sales of items
and help customers.
They manage the people who work for them.
They also pay bills.
The owners of music stores usually enjoy music.
They work with it all day long!

Farkle Fact

Today, many music stores allow customers to listen to
CDs before buying them. This makes it easy for people
to try new kinds of music.

Craftsman

Some people make musical
instruments by hand.
These people are craftsmen.
It takes many years for a craftsman
to learn how to make an instrument.
Many craftsmen also repair
musical instruments.
Sometimes, they are asked to make
a special custom-designed instrument
for someone.
Many craftsmen play the kind
of instrument that they build.
This helps them understand
how it should sound and work.

Farkle Fact

Antonio Stradivari made violins and other stringed
instruments in Italy during the 1600s and 1700s.
Today, a Stradivarius violin is worth millions of dollars.

Sound Engineer

Sound engineers must have
sharp ears when it comes to music.
They work behind the scenes,
rather than performing on stage.
Sound engineers work in **recording studios**,
helping musicians record their songs.
They set up microphones and choose
the right equipment.
They use computers to do the recording.
It is their job to work with musicians and
music producers to make sure that the song
sounds just right.

Farkle Fact

George Martin was the record producer for the famous
rock group the Beatles. He is known for the creative
things he did with music. Martin often added
orchestra instruments and sound effects to the
Beatles' rock-and-roll songs.

Music Teacher

Some musicians share their
love of music in a different way.
They teach music.
Elementary schools, high schools,
and colleges hire music teachers.
The teachers work with students
in the classroom.
Some music teachers also give private lessons.
They do this in their homes, at music stores,
or at their students' homes.
Music teachers prepare lessons for their students.
They may also spend time playing
their own musical instrument.

Farkle Fact

Joseph Haydn was a composer in the 1700s. He wrote
over 100 **symphonies**. Haydn was also a music teacher.
He had a student who became very famous—composer
Ludwig van Beethoven.

Other Musical Careers

There are many other jobs
in music.
Some people write music for movies
and television.
Session musicians work in a recording studio.
They play the background music
for vocalists and musical groups.
Some musicians play on city streets,
in department stores, or at festivals.
Other people like to write about music.
Music critics write about new CDs
and concerts.
All of these jobs need skilled and talented people.

Farkle Fact

Music therapists use music to help sick people feel
better. They work with both children and adults.

Think About It!

1. What does a sound engineer do?

2. Where might you find a music teacher?

3. Think of three things that a jazz musician does.

4. What is a conservatory?

5. With whom does an orchestra member practice?

The Story and You!

1. What steps would you take right now if you wanted to become a pop singer?

2. If you could do any of the jobs in this book, which one would you choose? Why?

3. Describe what you think it would feel like to perform on stage in front of thousands of cheering fans.

4. Do you know anyone that works in music? Think of five questions that you would like to ask him or her.

5. Pretend that you are a singer or musician on tour. You are traveling on a bus with your band, and you have been away from home for two months. Describe what you are thinking as you ride on the bus.

Vocabulary

audition–to try out for a performing job. *Dennis will audition for the symphony tomorrow.*

baton–a small wand used to direct a band or orchestra. *The conductor waved the baton through the air.*

conservatory–a school where music or dramatic art is taught. *Allison attended the conservatory to study the violin.*

harmony–a combination of sounds played together that are pleasing to the ear. *The instruments sounded in perfect harmony.*

jingle–a catchy song often used to advertise something. *The jingle for cat food was very funny.*

melody–musical notes that make a pleasing sound. *The song on the radio has a familiar melody.*

music producer–a person who manages the financial and creative decisions of how a record is made, sometimes called a *record producer*. *The music producer chose which songs would go on the record.*

pitch–the high or low sound of a musical instrument. *The flute has a higher pitch than all of the other instruments.*

score–music in a written format. *The conductor studied the score for the opera.*

recording studio–a specially designed room where records are made. *The singer went into the recording studio to record her album.*

symphony–a piece of music written for an orchestra. *Joseph Haydn wrote many symphonies.*

vocalist–a person who sings. *The vocalist sang five songs at the concert.*